Musings

370 Quick Hitting Thoughts for Life

Jeffrey Swarr

I.

The 21st Century is the age of information.

What can we do to move from an information-gatherer to an Action-Taker?

Take the great information available to you and turn it into action to make yourself better and to serve others, thus making the world better.

Write one thing down that you will do today...now go out and do it.

II.

Explore and know yourself. When you know yourself you have a foundation for decisions, choices, and ultimately your life

III.

Small things make a big difference. When you take the ordinary and add a little "extra" to it, you get the extraordinary. Do the Extra.

IV.

Look at and do what ought to be done; not because of the recognition you will receive for doing it, but because it is the right thing to do. When you train yourself to do this, we will do all the small things that need to be done.

V.

When we say, "Enjoy the journey." or "Trust the Process." It is not passive, but the potential to be actively pursued through study and physical work.

VI.

We must not accept the answers that first present themselves as the definitive answer. We must pursue deeper study of the questions, rather than settling for an immediate answer.

VII.

Take care of your physical condition not so you "look good," but so you need not rely on things outside of you or your control for your health.

VIII.

Be thankful to have a push toward growth and development of yourself, and not using time on that which you have no control over.

IX.

You are made for cooperation and connection. You are made to work together and connect with others. You are made to work with yourself, "opposable" thumbs are not opposing, but assisting.

X.

Regardless of the years you live, your life will be considered short if you are looking for the approval of others. You can live a full life by investing in your heart and soul.

XI.

What can be gained by working mindlessly, without thought? You injure yourself when you do anything without thought and engagement. You build yourself when you do even the smallest of things with the greatest of care.

XII.

Many people will live aimlessly wandering through life. When you train yourself to live with thought and engagement, you will live with intelligence.

XIII.

A second used thinking about others' opinions is a second wasted. Our activity should focus on our own path, only valuing the opinions of others that live in accordance with those values. This is not meant to be in a selfish way, but focusing on only what we control.

XIV.

While we are surrounded by others who might praise us and we might feel powerful as a result of this praise, it is up to us to do what is right and true to our Core Values.

XV.

You can elevate your mind by taking the time to reflect on each experience, each opportunity that is presented to you, not as good or bad, but as providing value to your life.

XVI.

If you can apply your right reason to what is right in front of you, with no expectations and no fear, you will live with the joy and happiness that no one can take from you.

XVII.

Do not wander through life. Live with a purpose and care for yourself. This is within your power.

⬚ XVIII.

Every act you undertake has a purpose. Know your values, reflect on your values, and live out your values in every action you take.

XIX.

The world around us is constantly changing and in order for us to live a full life, we must be solid in our values.

XX.

We shouldn't do something because it feels good or because it will enhance our reputation. We shall commit to action because we are fully convicted as it being aligned with our Core Values.

XXI.

When you concern yourself with others actions and thoughts, you bring strife into our lives. Living your life focused on what you think and do is to live a life of harmony.

XXII.

Do not desire fame when you are gone, because everyone will eventually pass. Enjoy the beauty of nature that is here for nature is what lives on.

XXIII.

We must ask ourselves, "Is this necessary?" While many interpret this as applying to tangible things, it also applies to our thoughts, actions, worries...Much of what we occupy our time with is unnecessary.

XXIV.

When we live in the past, we are paying for our experience.

When we are living in the future, we are borrowing to pay for our experience.

When we are present, we can profit from our experience.

XXV.

Nature and our experiences have built us, connect with nature, so as to build and give back to nature.

XXVI.

Work for wisdom, not that we can reach a goal or a destination, but a wisdom that we can share to serve and help others.

XXVII.

Remember that what we determine as our priorities are what we give our attention to. Live in accordance with your priorities and you will be grateful and live a full life.

XXVIII.

There are days to be endured and days in which we thrive, regardless of which it is, it is just a day, accept it as that and attack the next day.

XXIX.

The world loves change and while change is uncomfortable, change is constant. We are constantly changing, thus we will be constantly uncomfortable.

XXX.

Let yourself live fully without judging an event as good or bad, it just is.

XXXI.

Everything is connected. The events in our lives are connected as a series. The people in our lives are connected to the events. Recognize and appreciate these connections and these relationships.

XXXII.

Each day is a blessing. Each opportunity is a blessing. Each challenge is a blessing. We are blessed with nature. Living a life that appreciates each day, each opportunity, and nature is a blessing.

XXXIII.

Our blunders build us.

The burdens we bare are not the issue, it is in our view of these burdens that become the issue. To bare a burden with strength is a blessing...a burden builds us.

XXXIV.

There is much time behind us and much time in front of us, yet a small sliver of time in the present. Live fully in this little space called the present and we will fill the infinite space in front of us.

XXXV.

We are here in the world to be a human being, to appreciate all that is working together, to contribute to nature. Part of being human is to build in rest times, so you can refresh yourself, serving others, and eventually impacting the world.

XXXVI.

When we say, "Control the controllables," what does this mean? This is your effort over a period of time to do your work and the freedom to make choices that build on your control.

XXXVII.

Be content in the events in our lives because they are meant for us to use to live our destiny and know that we have the power to choose our response to these events.

XXXVIII.

There will be times when you make mistakes and you do not live in accordance with your values, you must not "beat yourself up" over this. You can learn from these times, gaining wisdom to apply in future events.

XXXIX.

A smooth pebble was once a rough, jagged rock. The pebble becomes smooth because it was driven by the turbulence of the water and so it is, you are shaped by turbulence and tumbles in your life.

XL.

We are here at this current place and time for good reason, so live in this moment, fully inhabiting the moment, and experiencing the moment.

XLI.

Our opponents may impact our action, but they cannot stop our thoughts, body language, or disposition.

XLII.

Your heart must not be pushed or pulled by the pleasure or pain that work brings upon you. Do not resist the work, do not label the work good or bad, it's just that, work. Engage in the work to the fullest.

XLIII.

Disagreement = Discovery

We must discuss our disagreements without anger, as anger takes away rational thought.

XLIV.

You can experience a full and happy life, when you refuse to be hindered by another person. Forgive others and allow justice to happen naturally to those you feel have wronged you.

XLV.

We are blessed with good fortune. Do not be drawn into the foolish world view to accrue objects or possessions. Good fortune is a healthy soul with actions that we control.

XLVI.

It has been said that the only constant in life is change. Everything in life does change, we change...either growing to become more or shrinking to be reduced to nothing.

XLVII.

"The best way of avenging yourself is not to become like the wrongdoer." - Marcus Aurelius

You will make mistakes, you will have regrets, you will do wrong to yourself. The one constant is our need to grow from these experiences.

XLVIII.

Keep your heart and soul in "shape" by choosing activities that nourish the heart and soul, choosing to associate yourself with those that have the same focus, yet coming in contact with those that will challenge your thoughts, so you can grow.

XLIX.

Forsake the desire for praise and favor coming from others, have your own mind, heart, and soul and you will bring contentedness and harmony into your life.

L.

Do not value the opinion or praise far away from you that you will never see. Value and build connections with those in close proximity to you.

LI.

We have the ability within our hearts to have no suspicion or hatred towards others, even those that have wronged you. This is not easy, but it is there for us to seize and act upon.

LII.

When it is proven that what we have done is in error, make an adjustment.

LIII.

Be on the lookout for the ways in which you can improve, taking pleasure in learning, especially in learning from others' experiences.

LIV.

Be adaptable to what happens to you and around you. Additionally be adaptable to the people around you, and most importantly, love those around you.

LV.

When we focus on what is within our control, we will love God and our fellow human beings. We know this because we will NOT judge God nor will we judge another as being good or bad.

LVI.

"Does the sun undertake to do the work of the rain…?" - Marcus Aurelius

When we live in accordance with nature, we understand that everything has a purpose AND we must allow nature to work in concert with each other. So it is true in our lives that each piece works together.

LVII.

If we experience something, it is "profitable" to us. If it is "profitable" to us, it is "profitable" to others. Be prepared to share your lessons.

LVIII.

Just because a person's name is known does not make them admirable. What makes a person admirable is their commitment to living a life in accordance with their values; treating those around them with love and respect.

LIX.

It is good to take notice of those around us, for we are surrounded by competitors that live by virtue and values. Take notice and align yourself with those that live in this fashion.

LX.

When you are faced with a barrier or obstacle that enters your way, remember this hindrance is merely a way for you to test your values.

LXI.

If it is not good for the TRIBE, it is not good for the individual.
If it is good for the TRIBE, it is good for the individual.

LXII.

There are things that happen in the world that have NO impact on your life. Do not be distracted by these events.

LXIII.

Every person has a passion. What fulfills your time will demonstrate your passion.

LXIV.

The actions we take will demonstrate our immediate intentions, but we must pay close attention to the words that give a window into our underlying beliefs.

LXV.

Look at your work. If you know someone who can do it better, let them do it. We should direct our energies towards such things that serve the good of the world, in this you will experience peace.

LXVI.

The connection of all things is special. This special connection forms order because each one of us serves a purpose.

LXVII.

The connection of all things is special. This special connection forms order because each one of us serves a purpose.

LXVIII.

"In a little while you will have forgotten everything; in a little while everything will have forgotten you?"

- Marcus Aurelius

Many things will happen in life that we will forget and many things we will do that others will forget. This can create freedom in our life to live it to the fullest, knowing that much will be forgotten.

LXIX.

Rather than worry about what you are lacking, focus on and be grateful for what you have. As we are grateful for these "things" we cannot put too much stock in them that we would miss them if they were gone.

LXX.

The weight of the wrongs done to us should be dropped immediately when it is thrust upon us, for it benefits us nothing to carry the weight of the wrongs against us.

LXXI.

We can work without complaining because we are so disciplined in our work and thoughts. As a result, we will be prepared to engage in the human experience to the fullest.

LXXII.

If you want to discover a treasure, you have to take the time to dig. Take the time to reflect, to study, to dig deep inside you and you will find the treasure that you are to share with the world.

LXXIII.

Make it so that you live a life in harmony with your values. Experience this harmony without any expectation that anyone other than yourself will recognize you for your harmony.

LXXIV.

We do our service, our good actions for it to be received by someone else, with no expectation of anything in return.

LXXV.

Be aware of your actions and their impact on others, but let go of the concern of how others will think about you. When you do this, you will live the life that you are intended to live.

LXXVI.

Our duty is to live the life of a good person, living with humility in who you are and a hunger to become more.

LXXVII.

It is important for you to take the time to check yourself and NOT work for fame or fortune. In this, you should also work to dismiss the ungrateful people that troll your life.

LXXVIII.

Everything that is important and should be done has a purpose. If you cannot find the purpose, then why are you doing it?

LXXIX.

Are you becoming something tomorrow or being something today?

There is a third option...Be something today, enjoy something today, engage in something today in order that you will become something even better tomorrow.

LXXX.

You have the power within yourself to be connected with your TRIBE. If you separate from your TRIBE, you can make a decision (choice) to come together with the TRIBE.

LXXXI.

When we strengthen our mind, are firm in our values and guiding principles, nothing can derail us. Be strong in your values and principles.

LXXXII.

Our judgment is within our control and we have the power to eliminate this judgment. For when we judge, we tend to complain. Eliminate the judgments, which eliminates the complaining. When we eliminate our complaining, we strengthen our power to act.

LXXXIII.

We have the opportunity to be a light unto others. Like the rays of the sun cutting through a hole in the clouds, be a light opening up the possibilities that exist for everyone.

LXXXIV.

We are put here in this place and time for one another. Every person we come in contact with is meant to be here; converse with them, break bread with them, engage with them. Build Connection.

LXXXV.

Are we seeking advice or are we looking for affirmation of our beliefs?

Seek the advice of others that have experience that you can learn from.

LXXXVI.

When you feel have been wronged by someone else, as difficult as it may be, it is not your role to right their wrong. Leave the wrong go, leave it be.

LXXXVII.

Evaluate your thought process in relation to the world, remembering that you are part of the world. Evaluate others to understand if their actions were out of lack of knowledge or with knowledge.

LXXXVIII.

We are part of a larger whole and all of our actions should be meant to support this TRIBE. When our actions do not support the TRIBE and our connection to the TRIBE, we are not living a FULL life, but living a fool's life.

LXXXIX.

Regardless of another's opinion of you, you would do well to be friendly with them. You can't go wrong when you treat others with care and respect.

XC.

If you follow each new thing that comes your way, you will constantly be ebbing and flowing; wandering without a core value or belief system. Living with core values provides a home base to come back to.

XCI.

Do what needs to be done and not because others will see your work. Do what needs to be done, even the simple and small without drawing attention to your work. As we do these simple and small things over time, others will notice your work.

XCII.

Do not pray that you will be blessed with this or that. Pray that you will see the opportunity to practice your purpose, living out your Core Values.

XCIII.

Regardless of your feelings regarding another person and their actions, they will not be removed from this world. You are given the power to oppose their actions and then let your feelings go.

XCIV.

Be intent and focused on what you are doing and how you are doing it. This is all you control, your work and how you go about doing this work.

XCV.

You are made to fight battles, to have adversity come your way. It does no good to complain, for the battle that you are fighting does not care about your opinion.

XCVI.

Mistakes and wrongs occur in our life. When you make a mistake, take ownership of it. When another person makes a mistake, make them aware of it and then let it go.

XCVII.

When you are part of something bigger than yourself, you will work for whatever is given to you that supports the mission of the larger TRIBE. You are called to what is helpful to the members of the TRIBE.

XCVIII.

Purpose, role, responsibility, or even your job signify what you are supposed to do or be. You must focus on your purpose and live out your purpose, not trying to be something else.

XCIX.

The world you live in is constantly changing and the people around you are constantly changing their beliefs. As a strong competitor your focus is on being true to your Core Values, living in the present, engaged in your work right in front of you.

C.

Our lives are NOT made up of the things we say we will do, but on the actions that we take.

CI.

When you allow fear or anger to invade your hearts and minds, it will take over all of your decisions and each second of your life. Develop the ability to recognize fear and anger, let them go and live with faith and joy.

CII.

How can you be offended by someone else's wrong when you have committed your own offenses?

Perfection is impossible. This is not a reason that you should lower your standards or be careless; you should have the perspective to understand wrongs will be done. Do not allow these wrongs to distract your focus from pursuing excellence.

CIII.

When compared to how long the Earth has been in existence, you are here for a brief time. Persevere and push through everything that is presented to you, living a full life in your time here.

CIV.

Whatever you do, do it to match your purpose. Make no excuses for living with purpose. You will never regret living out your purpose with passion. You will experience joy in living out your purpose.

CV.

If we look around us, all things are here for a brief existence. Nature produces seasons and buildings can be destroyed in an instant. Why get attached to that which is of a brief existence? Hold close the relationships you have established to engage fully in the time they exist.

CVI.

When you wish for things to be easy and for others to pat you on the back, you are robbing yourself of the opportunity to experience life. Fully experience that which occurs around you.

CVII.

Those that are without fault can be the first to point their finger at someone else.

Take the time to reflect on yourself first. Examine your words and actions first.

CVIII.

We are called to do good in this world. We can do good by having values and principles that guide us.

CIX.

Everything that you experience tells a story. If you are open to living and experiencing life, you can write the script.

CX.

When you treat someone else poorly, you are cutting yourself off from connecting with others, thus missing a part of yourself. You can treat others well, connect with others, thus allowing your own growth to occur.

CXI.

You will face obstacles in your path to live with steady progress. Be gentle toward these obstacles and do not allow these obstacles to make you act out of fear and turn you away from the path of daily progress.

CXII.

All activities will occur naturally because they follow nature. It is our focus to accept this nature and its activities. This sounds simple, yet it is not easy.

CXIII.

You will have wants and desires. You will have things to avoid and push away. When you can move to a mindset free of judgment, you can be free of desires and avoidance.

CXIV.

Honesty in all situations allows us to be free of guilt, shame, or second-guessing. Honesty need not be mean or vindictive, yet we can share the truth with love and care for our fellow competitor.

CXV.

Do we need to tell everyone about our character and about what we will do to support them?

Our actions will show those around us what is in our heart.

CXVI.

"This too shall pass." Seek out what is natural for you regardless of what it will get you.

Do what is good to serve the world that you come in contact with.

CXVII.

When you remove your judgment on an act, situation, or occurrence, you will get rid of any frustration about the situation. This is another reminder that you are meant to assess a situation based on facts, not on your judgment of it as good or bad, which is an opinion.

CXVIII.

We get more angst from our response to another's actions than the action itself. When we display anger, we will spend more time thinking of the anger than what caused the anger.

CXIX.

We must speak truth. Truth is what is in our heart. This honesty allows us to live a life that is honorable. Our delivery does not need to be rude or demeaning. In speaking the truth, we are able to solve the problems that are in front of us.

CXX.

Socrates felt the worst thing of all was to have had a person do a favor for him and not be able to return the favor.

Do not do something with the expectation of what you will get in return. Do something because you should do it and it being the right thing to do. Returning the favor will happen naturally.

CXXI.

You cannot help/serve others until you have first learned to help yourself. At first this sounds selfish, but the premise remains that you must first walk the way yourself before you can serve others on their journey.

CXXII.

As we progress (get older) we are moving to something that has not been created yet. When you are pushed, prodded, nudged in a direction, you are becoming a better version of yourself.

CXXIII.

Can you notice the past as a learning opportunity?

Can you trust in the future and that you will grow to become more?

Can you live in the present, enjoying where you are right now and not allowing another human's poor decision to become your poor decision?

CXXIV.

Because you have lived fully and competed in each moment, do not be afraid that at some point you will not be able to "play." KNowing that your career will end at some point should give us the freedom to compete.

CXXV.

Why do you place such an emphasis on another's opinion of you?

Stop looking for the approval of others; respect yourself, learn from others, and work to become the best version of yourself.

CXXVI.

Nobody else is responsible for our inner thoughts.

CXXVII.

Our greatest strength and power is to do God's will. Shout the praises of joy when you see his blessings AND accept the struggles that allow you to grow.

CXXVIII.

We are in control of our mind, let everything else happen as it may, but our mind is ours. Many things will happen around us or even to us, but to blame or give explanation is worthless. Save the time and energy that goes into blaming and explanation.

CXXXIX.

We have the strength within us to move from a person who impulsively reacts to a Competitor that mindfully responds. Impulsive reactions are focused on preserving yourself, while mindfully responding is engaging and doing what is best, even if it is NOT best for yourself.

CXXX.

Core Values and beliefs lead us through our life as the foundation for what we do. These Core Values and beliefs do NOT mean we need an opinion on everything, for the moment, we can relinquish our opinion, we can take hold of living in the moment.

CXXXI.

Every person plays an integral role in connecting in our lives, their intelligence and everything about them is a gift from God.

CXXXII.

Our lives will come to an end at some point, knowing this should push us to keep things simple, living a full life without boasting for the sake of pride.

CXXXIII.

There are so many parts of life that we see and many parts that are unseen. Our focus is to string these great experiences together recognizing the seen and acknowledging the unseen.

CXXXIV.

We are small!! We are one person in the billions that exist. We take up a small area of the vast size of the world. Our lives are short within the age of the Earth. While we are small and our life is short, we can have a huge impact on our lives, the number of people around us, and within the years we are living. Live fully.

CXXXV.

What is within our control? Our response to what occurs around us. We do not control when God decides our time is finished.

Marcus Aurelius noted, "...complete drama is determined by Him..." He then wraps up with this quote, "Depart then satisfied, for He also who releases you is satisfied."

Live your life in service to God and others.

CXXXVI.

When we make a decision to pursue something (Excellence, Greatness) it will take great effort and saying, "No" to many things, especially that which is not within your control.

CXXXVII.

Focus on and pursue that which is within your power.

CXXXVIII.

Average People -> Blame others for their situation

Good People -> Blame themselves for their situation and take responsibility

Great People -> Find no blame for any situation because blame does not change the situation, yet they take responsibility for the next step, executing a solution to the situation.

CXXXIX.

We can focus a lot of time wishing things to happen in a certain way or we can trust things will happen as we take the best action we can in the present moment, focusing on what we control.

CXL.

There will be barriers. The barriers are only physical barriers for us to overcome. The barrier is never a barrier to yourself and becoming the best you that you can possibly be.

CXLI.

The great question to ask about what happens around us is: How can we turn what is happening around us to greater develop a skill or to greater develop yourself?

CXLII.

It is better to end a season/year (die) with nothing (no championships) than to live with everything (championships) and be unsatisfied.

CXLIII.

If we desire to pursue goals outside of us and also adapt to what is happening around us, we will suffer.

This is the importance of having core values and knowing your purpose...You will have a north star that provides a guide on your path.

CXLIV.

When we want what others have and desire to avoid something, we are depending on someone else. We are choosing to be enslaved by these wants and desires. Choose to be free, focusing on what is within your control.

CXLV.

Pursue your passion with patience. Pursue your passion without pushing your desire to have it before the world is ready to put you in the right position.

CXLVI.

It is not what has happened to us that provides us discomfort, it is our opinion/judgment of what has happened that leads to our angst. We can show care to others that have experienced ills, yet we can not allow their suffering to become our suffering.

CXLVII.

We will do well to compete in our given situation while also looking at what we can learn from others.

CXLVIII.

Regardless of what the outcome is, you have the power to find a lesson and learn from the process. Do not allow the outcome to distract you from the lessons learned.

CXLIX.

It's easy for us to say focus on what you control, but this is difficult to do. Look at what is out of our control and Epictetus says we should, "despise" what is out of our control.

CL.

We will have many things that are done to us by others, but it is not what is done to us that insults us, it is our response/feelings about the other person that insults us. Allow there to be a time between the insult and our response and we will be Masters of our best life.

CLI.

When we keep in mind all of our fears and the worst possible outcome of death, we can focus on doing right by others.

CLII.

When we make a decision to live life by principles, outsiders will be unsure of how you do what you do. After they see your work, they will move to respecting you. Then they will move from respecting you to following your example.

CLIII.

When your focus begins to shift outside of you, know that you are moving away from your purpose. Your purpose is within your heart. Focus on the inside and you will dominate the outside.

CLIV.

Focusing on that which is within your power is the way to be the greatest asset and worth to your TRIBE.

CLV.

How do you respond when something happens to another? - Most times we show compassion and caring for others.

Can we respond the same way to the things that we experience? - Show compassion and caring to yourself.

CLVI.

When we take time to set up and identify our purpose, we will "hit the mark." When we take the time to listen to our heart our purpose will become clear and opportunities to live out this purpose will be presented.

CLVII.

When we are observing, seeing an action, ask yourself, "What happened before this?" then ask, "What happened after this?" There is more to an event, there is what leads to it and what is a result of it.

CLVIII.

It's simple, you will choose to be in control of your thoughts and actions or the outside world will control you. You can be like the pinball, pushed and shot everywhere or you can be focused on your purpose, driving your life through the world to bring your life to the fullness you deserve.

CLIX.

You may experience failure but you are not a failure unless you choose to view yourself as a failure. Make a choice to use failure as a learning tool to grow.

CLX.

Each experience provides the opportunity to learn to focus on what is within your control and what is within the control of a higher power. The higher power will put us in many situations (challenges), yet it is up to us to act.

CLXI.

Treat each day as its own, without expectation, not directing the day, but prepared to compete and move forward with whatever is given to you.

CLXII.

The more words we use the less power they have. 100 words = 1% per word.

The less words we use the more power they have. 10 words = 10% per word

CLXIII.

When you are given a hard time about your actions by another, remind them that you have many faults, not just those they are currently listing.

CLXIV.

When we take something on, be sure we are doing that "thing" not because it is "cool" or "feels good," but that we are aware of the experience and how we will be better from the experience.

CLXV.

When we undertake something, if it is right, do not concern yourself with others opinions that may be used to bring you down.

CLXVI.

Just as we take great care of our physical work to ensure safety, we must take great care of our mental and emotional well-being.

CLXVII.

Fill your mind with nourishment and stimulation at the beginning of your day and you will never be hungry.

CLXVIII.

Know that each person we come in contact with is doing their best with what they have. When we come in contact with them have compassion to help them get just a little bit better.

CLXIX.

We are not our possessions, we are so much more than that.

We are not our accomplishments, we are so much more than that.

We are who we choose to be in our heart, impacting and serving the world around us, there is nothing more than that.

CLXX.

Take what you have learned, share this learning with those that care to discuss, but only after you have listened to others.

CLXXI.

The person who holds you back is you. The only thing that keeps you back are your fears, doubts, questions, and insecurities that are lined up like an opponent ready to punch you in the face. Reach inside for the strength to fight back with your strength and commitment to become the best version of yourself.

CLXXII.

We are worthy!! We may not be where we want to be, but we have the opportunity to compete like we want to compete.

CLXXIII.

A life with many moving parts (complications) is difficult and short-lived. This doesn't mean it will kill you, but you can only carry on all the moving parts for so long.

Simplify your life and you will live long.

CLXXIV.

When we continue to live out our core values and grow, our life will be full to live.

CLXXV.

We are not and will never be perfect, however, our greatest asset is in our focus to acknowledge when we have done wrong.

CLXXVI.

Do you want to be respected by others?

Respect them first.

CLXXVII.

When we feel we are being controlled and have no choices, remember that no one can control our will.

CLXXVIII.

When we are connected with our heart, we are free to live. Connection with our heart is strengthened through our learning based on our daily experiences.

CLXXIX.

We are blessed with a number of challenges, yet we turn away from them.

Turn into the challenge and allow the challenge to create growth within you.

CLXXX.

Let your determination sets you apart.

Let your character set you apart.

Let your values set you apart.

Let your heart set you apart.

CLXXXI.

Physical fitness allows your body to perform and endure the elements. Mental fitness allows your mind to perform and endure the elements. You can work on both your physical and mental fitness for a healthy life.

CLXXXII.

Many people search for "things" to make them happy, which is an outside to inside approach. Happiness comes from your will, living in accordance with your values. This is an inside to outside approach. It all starts on the inside.

CLXXXIII.

All things are good in moderation. It is up to us to be present and engaged, which allows us to know the right amount of something. This is not about balance, it's about engagement.

CLXXXIV.

We can always be in control of our reasoned choice. We own our choices regardless of what is occurring around us.

CLXXXV.

Can we strive to become more yet live with satisfaction of where we are in the present?

This is a key to a fulfilled life.

Living for more, yet loving the present. Live to be more and Love who we are.

CLXXXVI.

It is not our situation that provides us with pain, but our pursuit of what we are missing that provides us with pain.

CLXXXVII.

Proper pride begins in the heart. Proper pride reminds us that our character and integrity are more important than our accomplishments.

CLXXXVIII.

Enjoying life and living well is a result of being able to determine the proper limit (moderation) of all things.

CLXXXIX.

When we gather together and break bread, we are building our body and our connection to others. What we eat will soon leave our body, yet what we gain in connecting with others will live within us for a longer time.

CXC.

Why waste time on anger? Anger is not effective and rarely ever changes anything...Anger hurts you and rarely helps you.

CXCI.

When we are active, some are calm. When we are calm, some are active.

In other words, life is a cycle that works together, not as a balance, but as a flow.

CXCII.

We will come in contact with those that we can learn from and those we can teach. It should be our focus to do both in our time together.

CXCIII.

Truths will come to light. Rather than being persuaded by opinion, focus on living in truth and seeking the truth.

CXCIV.

Living out Core Values does not mean you will always be victorious.

Living out Core Values means you will never be defeated.

CXCV.

To live freely is to release yourself from desiring more possessions. We can live to become more while at the same time appreciating what we are blessed with.

CXCVI.

Instead of gathering possessions, gather friends that refine you and push you to become the greatest version of yourself.

CXCVII.

When we connect with another person and raise them up, we are making an impact on generations to come. We make connections not out of selfishness, but out of love for one another.

CXCVIII.

We will be delighted with the occurrences in our life that happen sporadically and without warning or planning. Enjoy these events by being fully engaged in life.

CXCIX.

Our actions are considered good when they serve our purpose, making our mind, body, and soul stronger. If we make our mind, body, and soul stronger, we are bound to make those around us better.

CC.

Be slow to judge or condemn, yet quick to support and lift up.

CCI.

Will we ever regret forgiveness?

As you consider this question, can you recall a time where you should NOT have forgiven someone.

Perhaps the most important person to forgive is yourself.

CCII.

While there are great waves with a twisting and turning sea around us, we can be satisfied or find pleasure in being strong as the waves crash around us.

CCIII.

If you wish to leave a legacy and impact others, live with connection to others through being fair and just.

Serving others in their pursuit of excellence is to be fair and just.

CCIV.

You will do more for the world by helping build your heart and the hearts of those you come in contact with than building any physical structure. A physical structure will deteriorate, while the hearts of others will live on and build others up.

CCV.

Be more concerned with your character and integrity; what is in your heart, than the character and integrity of the structures around you. The structures will eventually need repair, while the heart lives through strength and connection.

CCVI.

Within every team, there will be those that are positive and committed combined with those attempting to find their way. Each member deserves the opportunity through discipline and progress to find their way to move the team forward to becoming a TRIBE.

CCVII.

Where there is good work to be done, you do it. Just as a rain shower provides nourishment and allows the plants to grow, you provide nourishment to those around you, allowing them to grow.

CCVIII.

The sailboat is not at the mercy of the wind. As the sailboat adjusts the sails to use the wind to move it forward, we must adjust our sails to respond to what happens around us, so we can move forward.

CCIX.

Our heart and soul must be conditioned and nurtured, for this is where our energy comes from. Just as the furnace requires fuel to heat the house, we must fuel our heart and soul to power our lives.

CCX.

Focus your life on virtues and values, for they will make your life richer than wealth.

CCXI.

Taking the time to think about what you say or do is a lost art. Create space between your thoughts and your actions or words for you cannot undo your words or actions.

CCXII.

We can give and receive feedback in a friendly and positive way, with care and love. In doing so, we are not judging the person, but we are connecting with them, so they know they are valued.

CCXIII.

When we help another person, it is not that specific person we are helping, but every person they can help. The impact is exponential.

CCXIV.

We will do many things that make us "happy" while we are doing them, and we regret them later. Great Competitors are able to resist these things and choose those things we don't enjoy doing, yet later on are happy we did them.

CCXV.

True freedom is the Mastery of yourself. Know who you are. Accept who you are. Be who you are. Enjoy who you are. Love who you are.

CCXVI.

Nourish your spirit each day. When you nourish your spirit you provide energy to yourself and those around you.

CCXVII.

God is always with us. If we can live with God being present in our lives, we will live a life that leaves a legacy.

CCXVIII.

Just as the sun rises in the morning, aids in the activity and growth around the world, and leaves in the evening, so do the challenges rise in our life, provide activity and growth in us, and these challenges leave our life.

CCXIX.

When our lives are advancing and prosperous, we will have many "friends." When we have struggles and challenges those that are present in our lives are true friends.

CCXX.

When we focus on what we do not have, we will experience sadness and sorrow. When we focus on the blessings that are present in our lives, we will experience more blessings.

CCXXI.

Release anger and hostility towards others by living the best life you can.

CCXXII.

As you move up in leadership positions and are saddled with increased responsibilities remember the number one responsibility is to connect with and care for those around you.

CCXXIII.

Be satisfied with the present or you will be considered foolish. When you are living in the present and enduring, you are demonstrating and building your strength as a Competitor in Life.

CCXXIV.

Being content in the present may be quick to experience, yet we will find the greatest joy in these moments of contentedness.

⁇

CCXXV.

To seek truth in any situation is a difficult endeavor, yet truth is what stands the test of time.

CCXXVI.

Teach lessons and provide instruction to your children and students, for their learning is more important than any riches we could provide for them.

CCXXVII.

Learning can take place anywhere and at anytime. Live to learn. Love to learn. Share your learning.

CCXXVIII.

Treat those around you well, so when they leave you, they will speak well of you.

CCXXIX.

Act as if...

When we look at what we want, we can act as if it already happened.

CCXXX.

Like a surfer rides the wave into the shore, we ride the challenges in our life until we reach the steady ground.

CCXXXI.

When we experience "bad luck" we must be reasonable, pause, and think clearly. "Bad luck" will occur, yet we must allow ourselves the opportunity to control our thinking and actions.

CCXXXII.

Our fellow man is fallible. When we can keep this in mind, we will never be amazed at anything that happens.

CCXXXIII.

God has placed us to where we are to focus on that which is within our power to impact. When we do this, we can live with freedom and happiness.

CCXXXIV.

Just because we have a certain education or connect with certain individuals, we do not earn a certain status by default of these relationships. In demonstrating our care for each other, we will lift the status of those around us and in turn our legacy will be built.

CCXXXV.

When we are content with where we are, we will experience fullness. Combine contentedness with the nudge to get better each day and we will have an unstoppable force.

CCXXXVI.

There are many concepts we will not understand in this world. We have been given the ability to know ourselves, so take the time to know who you are.

CCXXXVII.

Render powerless that which is not within your power.

CCXXXVIII.

Refuse to rank yourself. We are called to perform and play regardless of our rank or lot in life.

CCXXXIX.

"To be everywhere is to be nowhere." - Seneca

Be in the present. It's not about where you have been and it's not about where you are going. It's about where you are right now. We don't need to be everywhere, we just need to be right here.

CCXL.

"Regard him as loyal and you will make him loyal" - Seneca

Trust builds trust. When we display trust in those around us, we develop trust in those around us.

CCXLI.

We are given much, yet we are not satisfied. We have a full life, yet we feel an empty space. We have what is needed, yet we can never stop wanting. It is up to us to recognize what we are blessed with in our lives.

CCXLII.

We will look like others if our lives are only reviewed based on what our lives look like from the outside. On the inside is a different story, on the inside we are different, we are better than conforming to the masses.

CCXLIII.

As humans, our blessing of being able to project is also our greatest curse. When we stray from the present and project our worries to the future, this takes our worries of what "might" be, while we are robbing ourselves of what is right here in front of us.

CCXLIV.

Why focus on learning and improving?

Learning puts us in a position to teach. Nothing could be so selfish as to gain knowledge, experiences, and wisdom and hoard it to yourself.

CCXLV.

Be your own best friend. There is no substitute for pushing yourself, encouraging yourself because when you do this, you will be ready to impact and serve others.

CCXLVI.

Place yourself with people that will improve you.

Place yourself in positions where you have the opportunity to improve.

CCXLVII.

Don't do the work so as to be accepted by the crowd around you. Do your work so as to be accepted as who you are.

CCXLVIII.

Build your spirit, nourish you spirit, admire your spirit. Provide freedom to your spirit. Your spirit is your own, everything else that happens that is based on chance or good fortune is not owned, but rented.

CCXLIX.

Do you feel problems?

Not feeling the problem is a weakness.

Feeling the problem and overcoming it is the strength.

CCL.

The wise man is content with himself.

When you are content with yourself, you are bound to be at your best. You will reach out to others, you will connect with others because you are connected with yourself.

CCLI.

Being content with and knowing yourself is not stagnant or settling. Being content means you are comfortable with who you are presently, yet knowing you can become more.

CCLII.

Fools suffer from being dissatisfied with themselves and not recognizing the blessings around them and in their life. To be considered wise is to be content with what you have been blessed with.

CCLIII.

When we can influence a person's behavior without being present, we have made an impact.

CCLIV.

We have freedom of thought. Freedom to live without bounds and the requirements of someone else. Choose freedom from other's requirements and their expectations of and for you.

CCLV.

Nourish your mind. Nourish your spirit. Do these so you can grow as you get older.

You will be doing what Seneca says, "Cultivate an asset (the mind) which the passing of time improves."

CCLVI.

"The life of folly is empty of gratitude, full of anxiety; it is focused wholly on the future." - Seneca

Developing a practice of gratitude guides us to live a full and peaceful life.

CCLVII.

Maintain your spiritual enthusiasm, so as to always be building your spirit.

CCLVIII.

We will never please everyone. There will always be detractors.

CCLIX.

Fun times and experiences of success will prepare us for times of struggle. Times of struggle will prepare for the successes. Thus a cycle is in place to build your spirit through successes and rely on this spirit during the struggles.

CCLX.

In order to appreciate our riches, we must experience poverty.

CCLXI.

Experiencing anger allows us to appreciate the calm.

CCLXII.

Living and competing freely is a result of understanding that at some point we will not have the opportunity to compete. To understand that you will die/retire is to release you from the chains that you use to shackle yourself and that keep you from competing at our best.

CCLXIII.

"A good character is the only guarantee of everlasting, carefree happiness." - Seneca

Work on yourself, take care of yourself mentally, physically, and emotionally, because that is your only route to building happiness in your life.

CCLXIV.

You need reminders in your life. Why? You are human and can drift away from your purpose. You live in a society that tells you that you need more and are not enough. You need reminders because having a purpose needs to be deep in your being. You cannot hear or see your purpose too much.

CCLXV.

When we go to complain or look to move on from a situation, it's not the change in the scenery that we need, it's the change in our character that we need.

CLXVI.

The great life is available anywhere if you are open to developing it. Instead of running from here to there looking for something new and better, make the new and better inside yourself.

CCLXVII.

Our first step to developing is identifying that we have a need. Assess yourself.

Seneca writes, "Be harsh on yourself at times." I would add, "...be your own best friend."

Remember, best friends are honest.

CCLXVIII.

It is important that we read and gather information, and take quotes from others to learn and use in our life, however, the greatest impact is when we develop our own quotes to live by.

CCLXIX.

Are you imitating or creating?

Don't just puppet what others say or do, use your studies to develop your own quotes, your own stories, your own philosophy.

CCLXX.

There is benefit from talking together. The words do not have to be many, they just need to be impactful. Allow the mind to be open, to hear the words, allowing the words to be planted in our minds and grow.

CCLXXI.

How can you serve others, if you cannot take care of and nurture yourself?

CCLXXII.

It is not the quantity of words that are used, but the quality. It is not the speed at which we speak, but the connection of words to words.

CCLXXIII.

What's your purpose?

Seneca writes, "live in accordance with his [man's] own nature."

This is difficult because we push each other into processes other than living out our purpose.

CCLXXIV.

Receiving praise and having pride in something that is not yours is misguided. Own what is yours, your work, your actions, the rest is out of your control.

CCLXXV.

Honesty is the foundation that strong relationships are built upon. An honesty that is from the heart with concern for the heart of the other person.

CCLXXVI.

Connect with people around you, for if they do not speak in front of you, they will speak behind your back. Treat your inferior the way you want to be treated by your superior.

CCLXXVII.

Make your connections with people based on who they are rather than their social standing. Surround yourself with people with a good heart and as a group you will be lifted up.

CCLXXVIII.

We shall recognize that it will take more time to solve a problem than the time it took to create the problem. Stop looking for the "quick fix."

CCLXXIX.

Perhaps it is more important to learn what does NOT need to be done as it is to learn what is essential to do.

CCLXXX.

We aren't here to take what life (game) gives us. We are here to create a life that gives great joy. Joy through service. Joy through work. Joy through connection.

CCLXXXI.

Instead of trying to escape what is required, do what is required by choice and do it with enthusiasm.

CCLXXXII.

Be strong in your purpose. Persevere for your purpose. Be steadfast in your purpose.

CCLXXXIII.

Develop the ability to have an inactive mind. Busyness of the mind creates worry and anxiety. Create stillness while there is activity around you.

CCLXXXIV.

Death plays no favorites. Death can come at anytime. While we know this, do we live this? Live out a full life.

CCLXXXV.

In our lives we bring things to fruition. There is a reason these things that we focus on and think about actually occur. We place our energy into making them happen.

CCLXXXVI.

Are you like a soldier completing your term?

Or

Are you like an artist living out and creating your best life?

CCLXXXVII.

Living a full life with character, serving and impacting others makes the journey complete regardless of how long you live. Being a tribemate that connects with others, serves others, and builds the TRIBE, is a full life, regardless of your status.

CCLXXXVIII.

Living out your best life. This is written by many. Are you really living? We can truly live when we have established the idea of death (the end of our career) having no power over us.

CCLXXXIX.

Nourish your spirit. Work to build and maintain your physical health and in all the things you do, build your spirit. Our spirits lead us, support us, and move us from failure to success, and ultimately excellence.

CCXC.

When you encounter struggles remind yourself, "Even this will provide us with a good memory someday."

CCXCI.

Work for your goals because of what you can build on the inside (spirit, strength, heart) and not for the recognition (awards, networking) that you will receive on the outside.

CCXCII.

How would your actions change if there was an audience?

Be your own audience. Be the audience cheering on and providing the applause/energy to keep competing.

CCXCIII.

Life is full of variety. Recognize the variety, never giving into the adversity that will show up and never taking for granted the prosperity and good fortune that occurs in our lives.

CCXCIV.

Our lives are lived so there is nothing to hide. Nothing is hidden. While our neighbor or tribemate might not know everything about us, nothing is hidden from God.

CCXCV.

When we review our day, we can cement our learning and create a plan to use this learning in the future.

CCXCVI.

Wisdom is knowing the line that exists for us to enjoy our pleasures right up to the edge of where they can turn to a punishment.

CCXCVII.

Great Competitors are respected for their self-restraint to compete within a TRIBE and do what is required to complement the TRIBEmates...to have a sense of duty.

CCXCVIII.

Just as trees can be transplanted later in life, we can have an impact later in life. The older the tree the greater the shade. Live your life to build a greater reach.

CCXCIX.

Are you pursuing wisdom?

The pursuit of wisdom will set you free. The pursuit of wisdom will nourish your spirit and support all of your other studies.

CCC.

Keep on course!! There will be misfortune, bad luck, and things that will pull us off course. Stay the course, keep focused on living a life with values.

CCCI.

It's easy to measure possessions, money, outcome based things, but we mustn't focus on these things. We must focus on the tough to measure, the spirit. Build the spirit and soul that make up the Competitor.

CCCII.

Expecting nothing, yet prepared for everything.

True study is the study of yourself. Knowing yourself and being in control of yourself will provide more to your life than any other skill.

CCCIII.

Living a life of virtue and values requires time and effort. Create within your life the time and effort to build the virtues and values that lead to a life that is filled with character.

CCCIV.

Devote your attention to your life and how you live more than what you say. When you do this, your actions will do the talking.

CCCV.

Do your duty and will never be accused of abusing your power.

CCCVI.

We owe the power we have to those in which we have power over. (True for parents, coaches, teachers, leaders...everyone.)

CCCVII.

All progression is possible as a result of study. The opportunity to think, evaluate, reflect and then to use this study to make adjustments or develop something new.

CCCVIII.

Honor, integrity, and character are priceless. These three are never for sale and cannot be bought.

CCCIX.

You can live in harmony with nature and what will naturally happen. When you live in harmony, you can care as much about another person as you do about yourself.

CCCX.

Virtues and character are developed. We are born with the ability to develop virtue, the tools to be virtuous. Like a farmer cultivating his crops, virtue and character are the result of the work on the ground.

CCCXI.

Growing something takes time. Some may say it is a "process." We must be on guard, as this process can be undone in seconds. This daily work and routine is essential, so as to never let this process go to chance.

CCCXII.

A setback has often cleared the way for greater prosperity.
Our setbacks, the disintegration of what we have built, will
often lead to even greater prosperity.

CCCXIII.

Fortune and the world around us provides no distinction or
care as to our name or fame. No one is greater than another.
Death does not discriminate, so we should not.

CCCXIV.

We can work to be in control of our mind, being able to focus
with a solitary mind when much is going on around us.

CCCXV.

You are put here to live!! You make choices that keep you back. You make choices that lead to the death of yourself. Make the choice to live, free of any fears. Make the choice to Compete and Get After It.

CCCXVI.

It has been said that we can't run from our problems. Our problems run with us. They run with us because we don't take the time to nourish our spirit. Reading, studying, and growing is nourishing to our spirit.

CCCXVII.

You can't run from yourself. Invest the time in yourself. Rid yourself of the heavy load. Rid yourself of the burdens that weigh you down.

CCCXVIII.

Don't be concerned by what the future may bring, be strong and prepared for whatever fate will thrust upon you.

CCCXIX.

Search not for safety, but risk. This is the life we are meant to live, using our ambition to become more, to expect more, to serve more. These are the risks to take that lead to living with honor.

CCCXX.

That which is hard in our life does not cause us to lose our confidence. We make it hard because we lack the confidence to attack that which is hard. Attack the impossible.

CCCXXI.

Sacrifice leads us to freedom. To live freely we are called to make sacrifices. Sacrifices of yourself and you will receive freedom from the expectation to do everything.

CCCXXII.

Be at peace with yourself and those around you.

CCCXXIII.

"...talking with other people as little as possible, with yourself as much as possible." - Seneca

Focus on conversation with yourself to know who and what you are.

CCCXXIV.

The man that lives with respect for their fellow man
(opponents) will live a life free of guilt.

CCCXXV.

Nothing will take us by surprise. This life is a rugged journey
and constant reflection ensures the fact that no struggle will
take us by surprise.

CCCXXVI.

Live with a noble spirit. A spirit that brings us to a place of
peace with all that we encounter, remembering that our
spirit rides the waves of the ups and downs that fortune will
present before us.

CCCXXVII.

"It is what it is."

We would do well to endure what we are experiencing as what was destined to happen without complaint.

CCCXXVIII.

Trusting in the hands of fate is difficult, yet freeing. Trusting in the hands of fate means changing yourself, so you can trust fate.

CCCXXIX.

"The more the mind takes in, the more it expands." - Seneca

Provide yourself with experiences and opportunities to learn, for the more opportunities you have, the more you will grow.

CCCXXX.

What you have is enough. Being enough without being complacent. Compete in the present, being right here, right now, with what you have, allowing this current situation to help you become more.

CCCXXXI.

You can always do something with nothing. When we want for nothing, we will be blessed with something and know that we have everything we need.

CCCXXXII.

When we use fear to motivate, it's an illusion that progress is being made and goals are being met.

Choose to motivate and inspire with faith.

CCCXXXIII.

Our days fly by, carrying us here and there. Be the pilot of your days, rather than ending up as a passenger for years.

CCCXXXIV.

When you consider yourself "old" you will act in accordance with being old. Keep yourself young by living each day as your best day.

CCCXXXV.

May your words become your works. Allow your words to lead you to great works, impacting others and in the process creating a lasting legacy.

CCCXXXVI.

Ride the waves in your life. Like the surfer that steadies the mind and body as the waves ebb and flow, we must steady our self and connect with life, turning our words into our works.

CCCXXXVII.

When our spirit has energy and is alive, our actions will be brisk.

CCCXXXVIII.

How do you handle prosperity? Do you allow prosperity to change who you are? What has allowed you to prosper?

CCCXXXIX.

Our faults are connected to our values. Our values are connected to our faults.

CCCXL.

We get our demeanor (way we carry ourselves) from our spirit. Nurture your spirit so as to keep your spirit strong.

CCCXLI.

Live to see the sunrise, being prepared to work and live life. Living while the sun is up and resting while the sun is down.

CCCXLII.

Pull out the satisfaction in the usual. Take pleasure in having a routine. As hectic as this world is, take solace in the fact that you are strong enough to build a routine.

CCCXLIII.

Doing what is right is simple. Doing what is wrong is complex. Stay simple. Living simple is uncommon in this utterly complex world.

CCCXLIV.

We have within our power the ability to get used to living with little. Take the little that you have and do the most with it.

CCCXLV.

Don't be seduced or pulled in by convention. Because other people do it, does not make it acceptable. The only way to develop happiness in life is to live life and live it to the fullest.

CCCXLVI.

We will have a tendency to avoid hard work, pain, struggle; do not be afraid of these, for they will lead us to the advancement we truly desire.

CCCXLVII.

There is no limit to what we can learn, yet there is a limit to what we can recall.

CCCXLVIII.

We can only offer counsel on that which is within our control, that which we have the power over to act.

CCCXLIX.

We all have a certain end in mind...the freedom of choice. We have the power to choose what to do and what NOT to do.

⍰

CCCL.

Our wealth is not determined by what we own. Our wealth is shown by what we do with what we have.

CCCLI.

Do you attempt to do what is good for another? This is being a friend, doing what is good for another.

CCCLII.

We are reminded to build on the good, bring the good into our lives while we lessen and eliminate the bad.

CCCLIII.

Actions done selflessly for others are noble. (The idea of selfish living has been around for thousands of years. It is part of human nature to battle the idea of being selfish.)

CCCLIV.

Praise others for their good deeds. Praise others when we believe they are able to do good. So it should be said, "Praise others."

CCCLV.

When we act out of revenge, we are acting merely for our own selfish feelings.

CCCLVI.

"For where there is competition, there is victory." - Aristotle

When we compete, we will be victorious. Compete in everything you do, leads to victory in everything you do.

CCCLVII.

The root of many wrongs is jealousy.

We end up wanting what someone else has.

Be content with what you are gifted.

CCCLVIII.

It is easy for us to act out of emotion. It is easy for us to act out of anger. It is difficult to take a breathe and allow emotions to subside before acting.

CCCLIX.

When we take the initiative to do things without being asked AND do NOT proclaim our own good works after they are completed is the highest form of friendship or selflessness.

CCCLX.

When going through tough and undesirable times, remember you are learning something that you can use in the future.

CCCLXI.

As part of a TRIBE remember: Everyone wants to do the job. Mission accomplishment requires everyone's effort. Believe all members can be trusted.

CCCLXII.

The only purpose we can undertake is to be as good as we can possibly be. When we work to be as good as we can possibly be, we do this with an intense disregard for success or failure.

CCCLXIII.

The most difficult thing you can do on your journey is to overcome your focus on yourself.

⸮

CCCLXIV.

Acknowledging what we don't know is more important than acknowledging what we do know.

CCCLXV.

Consider new ways to do the old. As things change around us, take the time to use what we already know and apply it in new ways

CCCLXVI.

Be so full of joy and energy in your work that you forget your worries.

CCCLXVII.

When you allow yourself to trust others or engage in self-sacrificing behavior/choices, you foster a connection to something bigger than yourself.

CCCLXVIII.

3 Simple Rules to live by:

Do your best for everyone.

Be trustworthy in what you say.

When you make a mistake, take responsibility for it and make a change.

CCCLXIX.

What good is it to align yourself with people that agree with everything you say?

In order to grow, your thoughts must be challenged.

CCCLXX.

Engage in your journey aware of what nature provides to you and will live a full life.